D1192703

THE RISE OF ANIME AND MANGA

From Japanese Art Form to Global Phenomenon

Bradley Steffens

ReferencePoint
Press®

San Diego, CA

© 2024 ReferencePoint Press, Inc.
Printed in the United States

For more information, contact:
ReferencePoint Press, Inc.
PO Box 27779
San Diego, CA 92198
www.ReferencePointPress.com

LIBRARY OF CONGRESS CATALOGING-IN-PUBLICATION DATA

Names: Steffens, Bradley, 1955- author.
Title: The rise of anime and manga : from Japanese art form to global
   phenomenon / by Bradley Steffens.
Description: San Diego, CA : ReferencePoint Press, 2024. | Includes
   bibliographical references and index.
Identifiers: LCCN 2023019039 (print) | LCCN 2023019040 (ebook) | ISBN
   9781678205867 (library binding) | ISBN 9781678205874 (ebook)
Subjects: LCSH: Manga (Comic books)--Japan--Juvenile literature. | Manga
   (Comic books)--United States--Juvenile literature. | Manga (Comic
   books)--Influence--Juvenile literature. | Animated
   films--Japan--Juvenile literature. | Animated films--United
   States--Juvenile literature. | Animated television
   programs--Japan--Juvenile literature. | Animated television
   programs--United States--Juvenile literature. | LCGFT: Comics criticism.
   | Film criticism. | Television criticism and reviews.
Classification: LCC PN6790.J3 S74 2024 (print) | LCC PN6790.J3 (ebook) |
   DDC 741.5/952--dc23/eng/20230424
LC record available at https://lccn.loc.gov/2023019039
LC ebook record available at https://lccn.loc.gov/2023019040

CONTENTS

A Niche No More

On November 24, 2022, the revelers lining the streets of downtown New York for the ninety-sixth Macy's Thanksgiving Day Parade saw something unusual floating above the crowd—a giant, muscular cartoon character with wild, light blue hair. It was a balloon depicting Son Goku, the hero of *Dragon Ball*, a popular series of both Japanese graphic novels, known as manga, and animated films, known as anime. Balloons depicting manga or anime characters were not traditionally featured in the Macy's parade, but beginning in 2018, when Son Goku made his first appearance, they have been making their way down the parade route along with American cartoon characters, including Mickey Mouse, Scooby-Doo, and Snoopy.

Ready for Prime Time

The presence of Son Goku was a tribute to the growing popularity of manga and anime in the United States. According to the online trade magazine ICv2, the sales of manga books in the United States topped 24 million copies in 2021—an increase of 160 percent over the previous year. The video streaming service Netflix reports that more than half of its subscribers watched some anime on the platform in 2021. "It's becoming less of a niche thing, especially now that Netflix picked up a bunch [of shows]," says Kevin Xue, tech chair for Northwestern University's anime club. "I think that was a really big turning point in terms of people starting to watch it because everyone has Netflix."[1]

Anxious to feed America's growing appetite for anime, Netflix developed eight original series for 2023, including *Akuma-kun*, the story of a youthful messiah who tries to bring about peace and harmony in the world by harnessing the power of demons. The adaptation of *Akuma-kun* is new, but the manga debuted in 1963, making it one of the longest-running fictional series in Japan.

Video streaming service Crunchyroll also released a bevy of new anime programs in 2023, including the final installments of *Attack on Titan*, a series about the last survivors of the human race living in a walled city besieged by gigantic human-eating humanoids known as titans. Based on a manga series by Hajime Isayama, *Attack on Titan* was the most in-demand program in the United States for three weeks in 2021 and was the most in-demand television series in the world for all of 2021, according

A huge balloon depicting Son Goku—the muscular, blue-haired hero of the popular Dragon Ball *series—thrills spectators at the 2021 Macy's Thanksgiving Day Parade in New York City.*

to the market research firm Parrot Analytics. One reason for the show's popularity is the nail-biting danger humans face in every episode. "*Attack on Titan* is the only thing I have ever watched where I would literally shout warnings at the screen,"[2] says Jaryd Garcia, a thirty-year-old marketing coordinator in Norwalk, California.

Dedicated Fans

Garcia and his anime-loving coworkers were so anxious to see what happened next in *Attack on Titan* that they would stream the latest episodes as soon as Crunchyroll released them in the United States, just an hour after they aired in Japan. Unfortunately for Garcia and his coworkers, the releases occurred in the middle of the workday. "Part of my job was to greet visitors to the office," Garcia says. "When a new episode of *Attack on Titan* would drop, we would take our lunch break and watch it. I couldn't lock the front door, but I would dim the lights in the reception area, hoping that people would think the office was closed so we wouldn't be disturbed."[3]

Garcia's enthusiasm for manga and anime is not that unusual. In fact, the Japanese have a word for it: *otaku*. Coined in 1983 by columnist and editor Akio Nakamori, *otaku* describes people with consuming interests, particularly in manga, anime, video games, or computers, often to the detriment of their social skills. Although used in a critical sense to describe Japanese people who are not quite acting as adults, *otaku* is an affectionate term for people outside the island nation who love Japanese products, art forms, and culture.

Erasing the Stigma

Until recently, manga and anime had a stigma in the United States as well. "This sounds so mean, but the people I knew in middle school that were into it were kind of weird, and some of the anime I had seen also seemed really out there," says Allison Rauch, a student at the Medill School of Journalism, Media, Integrated Marketing Communications in Illinois. Recently, however, Rauch became hooked on *The Disastrous Life of Saiki K*, an anime comedy about a high school student with psychic abilities who wants to keep his powers secret. "Saiki K, I love that kind of satirical humor," says Rauch. "I think through giving the genre a try I've been able to find stuff I really like."[4]

Rauch's story is being repeated on a global scale. According to research firm Ampere Consumer, 2.88 billion people—36 percent of the world's population—watched at least some anime in 2021. That is a 50 percent increase from 2018, when 24 percent of viewers enjoyed the Japanese animated movies and TV shows. Anime has broken out of its niche. "For anyone who was trying to be a hipster and watch anime because it wasn't mainstream, it's a terrible thing," says Northwestern University student Antony Traino. "Now you get a lot more widespread acknowledgement that it's a real art form and not just some fringe media."[5]

"For anyone who was trying to be a hipster and watch anime because it wasn't mainstream, it's a terrible thing. Now you get a lot more widespread acknowledgement that it's a real art form and not just some fringe media."[5]

—Antony Traino, student at Northwestern University

CHAPTER ONE

The Origins of an Art Form

While manga and anime are relatively new art forms, their roots go back several centuries. They borrow elements from medieval Buddhist scrolls, eighteenth-century block prints, nineteenth-century newspaper cartoons, Japanese theater, and puppet shows. These diverse forms influenced manga and anime artists to work in a highly stylized and instantly recognizable manner.

Manga and anime tell stories in words and pictures, with the pictures dominating the medium. The earliest surviving examples of this technique are sets of paper scrolls created in the twelfth century by Buddhist monks. The scrolls were up to 46 feet (14 m) long and about 1 foot (30.5 cm) high. The reader would unwind the scroll with one hand and re-wind it with the other, leaving an approximately 24-inch (61 cm) reading panel between the two sides.

Stories in Pictures

The oldest surviving scrolls of this type are the *Chōjū giga* (*Scroll of Frolicking Animals*). The four scrolls, each 11 to 13 yards (10.1 to 11.9 m) in length, were housed at the Kōzan-ji Buddhist temple in Kyoto, Japan, and were likely created by Buddhist monks living there around 1150. The scrolls are often attributed to the artist-monk Kakuyū, also known as Toba Sōjō (Bishop of Toba), but British historian George Bailey Sansom dismisses this idea, in part because Kakuyū lived in Toba and died before the scrolls were completed. Whoever the artist or artists were, their lighthearted touch embodied "the artistic spirit of their age," writes Sansom. "In general, religious painting tended to resemble secular painting in its attitude. The lofty and severe gave way to the tender and graceful. . . . The artist is a delightful draughtsman. His pictures of animals disporting [frolicking] in the garb of monks are alive with satirical fun."[6]

Drawn in black ink without color, the *Chōjū giga* scrolls depict rabbits, frogs, and monkeys behaving like humans. The opening scene shows rabbits and monkeys frolicking in a body of water. A later scene presents frogs and rabbits competing in an archery tournament. Another shows them engaged in sumo wrestling. In one scene rabbits and frogs with long sticks chase after a monkey that has stolen something. Reflecting the religious character of the scrolls, the final scene of the first scroll

Although manga and anime sometimes use words to tell stories, they use illustrated pictures more often. This technique can be seen in Scroll of Frolicking Animals (pictured), thought to have been created by Buddhist monks around 1150.

shows a monkey dressed as a priest presenting an offering to a fat frog seated on a lotus leaf throne—a playful representation of the Buddha.

Because the *Chōjū giga* scrolls tell stories in pictures, many people consider them to be the first manga. However, the whimsical pictures are not accompanied by any text. For this reason, manga artist Seiki Hosokibara disputes the idea that *Chōjū giga* is the forerunner of manga. The *Chōjū giga* scrolls do, however, embody some of the features of modern anime, in which the story's words seldom if ever appear on the screen. Sometimes as the reader unwinds a *Chōjū giga* scroll, a large scene passes through the viewing area, an effect later duplicated in anime by a camera panning across a landscape or cityscape. Similarly, the *Chōjū giga* characters pass across the viewing area of the scroll as if in action. The ancient story was probably spoken aloud as the reader turned the scrolls, adding a voice-over or soundtrack to the visual presentation, as in anime.

Pictures and Words

While acknowledging *Chōjū giga* as a masterpiece of illustration, Hosokibara points to a late twelfth-century scroll, *Shigisan Engi Emaki* (*Legend of Mount Shigi Emaki*), as the first true manga. Like *Chōjū giga*, *Shigisan Engi Emaki* consists of paper scrolls illustrated in a horizontal format. There are three *Shigisan Engi Emaki* scrolls, each about 12.5 inches (31.7 cm) high. One scroll is about 28 feet (8.5 m) long, one is 41 feet long (12.5 cm), and one is 46 feet (14 m) long. Unlike the *Chōjū giga* scrolls, the *Shigisan Engi Emaki* scrolls tell the stories in both pictures and words, with hand-painted calligraphy in between the illustrations. In addition, the artist or artists who made the *Shigisan Engi Emaki* scrolls created the ink drawings with colorful vegetable dyes, making them look more like today's manga drawings.

More importantly, perhaps, the story told in the *Shigisan Engi Emaki* scrolls is a genuine precursor of manga and anime works. The narrative is truly epic. It includes fantastical scenes

Interpreting Chōjū giga

Because the drawings of *Chōjū giga* (*Scroll of Frolicking Animals*) are not accompanied by text, the precise meaning of the scroll has been lost to time. In the excerpt below, scholars at the University of Colorado discuss the scroll's possible meaning.

Many theories exist to explain why this scroll was painted. It may have been created simply for entertainment, as a commentary on Buddhist rituals, or as a satire on court and religious life. Some think the scroll is commenting on the changes in the late Heian period [794 to 1185]. The exquisite high culture of the nobility was losing control of the government as the warrior class was gaining power. Competition between different Buddhist sects had seen warring monks competing for power. During this time, there was an increase in Buddhist ceremonies and rituals to honor the imperial family and to protect its well-being. These rituals were performed to insure the power and interests of imperial control. The ceremonial rituals were possibly the target for parody and satire in the *Chōjū giga*. . . . In many periods of history, humor, satire, and parody have been used to express concern about political, social, economic, and cultural changes.

Ethan Segal and Jaye Zola, "A Case Study of Heian Japan Through Art: Japan's Four Great Emaki," Program for Teaching East Asia, University of Colorado, 2008. www.colorado.edu.

that would not be out of place in a modern-day manga book or anime movie. The scroll tells the story of Myōren, a Buddhist monk who lived at the end of the ninth century in the Shigisan Chogosonshi-ji Temple, high on Mount Shigi in Nara Prefecture. The first scroll, *The Flying Granary*, tells of Myōren's incredible ability to make objects levitate, using nothing but the power of his mind. Every day Myōren would send his rice bowl flying down the mountain to a granary tended by a wealthy farmer. The farmer would fill the bowl with rice, and Myōren would fly the bowl back up the mountain so he could eat. One day the farmer refused to fill the bowl for Myōren. To punish the farmer for his selfishness, Myōren flew the entire granary up the mountain. When the farmer came to beg forgiveness, Myōren sent sacks of rice flying out of the granary and through the countryside to the families below, who watched in amazement as sacks of rice sailed overhead.

While the creator of the *Shigisan Engi Emaki* scrolls told the tales in words, the text was interposed between the drawings. By contrast, the anonymous artist who created a sixteenth-century scroll, *Saru no sōshi* (*Illustrated Tale of Monkeys*), placed the text in and around the illustrations, as manga artists do today. The drawings even include the first known speech bubbles to indicate who is talking. Like *Chōjū giga*, *Saru no sōshi* belongs to a genre of Japanese works known as *irui-mono*—stories acted out by animals. In this case the scroll shows monkeys in human situations, both serious and comical. The scroll describes the entertainment that Prince Shizubane of the Hie Shrine provides to Yoshinari Yasaburo, his prospective son-in-law. The Hie Shrine is an important Shinto shrine dedicated to the deity Oyamakui-no-kami, whose

Origins of the Word *Manga*

Most historians credit Katsushika Hokusai with coining the word *manga* as a portmanteau of the Japanese words *man* ("whimsical") and *ga* ("picture"). However, Hirohito Miyamoto of Meiji University in Tokyo argues that the word's history may be more complicated than that.

The Sino-Japanese word "manga" originally referred to a type of bird called a spoonbill, and there are examples of such usage in Japan starting in the early 18th century. . . . Starting around the end of the 18th century, we started to see examples of the word being used to mean free-spirited drawings, but the term still didn't mean humorous caricatures. The word manga in the "Hokusai Manga" [Hokusai's Sketches], a series of works by the . . . artist Hokusai Katsushika, is an example of this . . . usage.

There are two theories on the meaning of manga as it is used in the title "Hokusai Manga": one is that it refers to the free-spirited nature of the drawings, and the second is that—like the spoonbill, which tirelessly hunts all day long in search of food—the drawings cover a diverse range of subjects and are depicted using a diverse range of techniques.

Hirohito Miyamoto, "Is This the First Manga?," Google Arts & Culture, 2020. https://artsand culture.google.com.

divine messengers are monkeys. This is why the characters in the tale all appear as monkeys. Dressed in bright clothing, the simian characters are shown feasting and taking part in the classic Japanese tea ceremony. The scroll also provides the earliest known illustration of a *renga* poetry meeting, in which each participant composes a short poem linked to the poems before it, creating one long poem. In addition to the fantasy element, the illustrations in the *Saru no sōshi* feature other techniques found in modern manga, including strong visual action, amusing details, and the dominance of pictures over words.

Naming a Style

In the 1700s scrolls gave way to printed books that told comic stories in words and pictures. In 1814 the artist Katsushika Hokusai coined the word *manga* from the Japanese words *man*, meaning "whimsical," and *ga*, meaning "picture," for the title of a series of illustrated books depicting scenes from everyday life. Hokusai's works did not tell stories, but his ability to create humorous, vivid characters with simple drawings influenced artists for generations to come.

In the middle of the nineteenth century, after centuries of remaining closed to the West, Japan began to open trade with Europe and the Americas. The country began to be influenced by Western culture as well, including an interest in newspapers and magazines. In 1862 the English artist and cartoonist Charles Wirgman, who was living in Yokohama, began to publish and illustrate *Japan Punch*, a satirical magazine modeled after the famous British magazine *Punch*. The Western cartoon style influenced many Japanese artists, including Kitazawa Rakuten, who began to publish a humorous newspaper called *Jiji Manga* (*Topical Manga*) in 1902. Kitazawa decided to illustrate the French short film *The Waterer Watered* as a series of panel drawings, creating what many people recognized as the first modern manga. In addition to reviving Hokusai's term, *manga*, in the title of his newspaper, Kitazawa also coined the word *mangaka* to describe himself as a manga artist—a term that manga creators still use today.

The Advent of Anime

Just as manga was influenced by Western aesthetics, so too was anime. Émile Cohl's 1908 film *Fantasmagorie*, considered by film historians to be the first animated cartoon, fascinated Japanese artists. Winsor McCay's 1914 film *Gertie the Dinosaur*, which combined live-action scenes with animated ones featuring the title character, a fancifully drawn apatosaurus, also captivated Japanese filmmakers. Three artists, Ōten Shimokawa, Jun'ichi Kōuchi, and Seitarō Kitayama—collectively known as the "fathers of anime"—began to make their own animated films. The earliest surviving of these is Kōuchi's 1917 film *Namakura Gatana* (*The Dull Sword*), the only remaining copy of which was discovered in an Osaka antique store in 2008. The two-minute silent film tells the story of a self-styled samurai who is tricked into buying a dull-edged sword. He engages in the traditional practice of *tsujigiri* ("crossroads killing"), testing the effectiveness of his new weapon by attacking human opponents, only to be easily defeated by his would-be victims in a series of comic episodes. "It was an era when people were surprised just to see that the pictures moved," says Yoshiro Irie, a researcher at Tokyo's National Film Center. "The films are also full of gags."[7]

One of the other few surviving films from this era is Kitayama's 1918 film *Momotarō* (*Peach Boy*). Based on a fourteenth-century folktale, *Momotarō* tells the story of baby discovered in a peach that an old woman finds floating down a river. The child, Momotarō, explained that he was given to the childless woman and her husband by the gods. As he grew, Momotarō showed remarkable strength, cutting down a large tree with a knife when he was just five years old. As a teenager, Momotarō battled demons and ogres that were devastating the land.

The story of Momotarō continued to be adapted by various mangaka and

> "It was an era when people were surprised just to see that the pictures moved. The films are also full of gags."[7]
>
> —Yoshiro Irie, researcher at Tokyo's National Film Center

The fourteenth-century folktale Momotarō (Peach Boy) has been adapted into manga and anime. Pictured is an illustration from the story. The illustration appears in a book of Japanese myths and legends.

anime filmmakers. During World War II, the Japanese hero was used for propaganda purposes. Momotarō was shown battling the Western Allies, including the United States, which were presented as *oni*, or evil spirits.

A Need for Escapism

After World War II, with many of Japan's cities decimated and money scarce, Japanese publishers began to produce cheaply printed manga books with mostly red covers. These low-cost books, known as *akahon*, or "red books," were sold at roadside stands. A new generation of artists began to fill the need for the illustrated stories.

Having witnessed the horrors of mechanized warfare—including the first use of nuclear weapons, which incinerated the Japanese cities of Hiroshima and Nagasaki—the young Japanese mangaka spurned realism in favor of escapist fare. They retold stories from Japanese folklore, replete with spirits, demons, and talking animals. They also illustrated European fairy tales, including *The Little Mermaid*, *Snow White*, and *Puss in Boots*. They even adapted escapist Western novels as manga books. One of these, *New Treasure Island* by Osamu Tezuka and Sakai Shichima, sold four hundred thousand copies as a red book.

Inventing a Style

During World War II, the film industry was pressed into service to support the war effort. Afterward, Japanese film studios returned to producing pure entertainment. Some studios wanted to produce animated features like those made by America's Walt Disney Studios. However, because of a lack of capital, the movies had to be made on tight budgets. Japanese animation companies could not produce the high number of individually drawn sheets of celluloid, or cels, that Disney used in its animation. Typically, Disney photographed twenty-four different cels for every second of the motion picture. The changes from one cel to the next were small, and when they ran at normal speed, the motion they depicted looked fluid. This technique is known as full animation. However, the Japanese studios could not afford to draw twenty-four cels for each second of a film. They settled on using eight cels per second. They also tried to limit the changes from cel to cel—a technique known as limited animation. For example, to express emotion, Japanese animators borrowed a technique from street puppetry, in which the puppeteer changes the puppet's expression by adjusting only the eyes, eyebrows, and mouth. By changing only these parts of the expression, the animators could show emotion without redrawing the entire face. They might narrow the

Unlike early Disney animators, who worked with large numbers of cels, early Japanese animators had a limited supply. The result was an altogether different style of animation. Pictured is an example of a cel, this one from the 1982 animated television film The Snowman.

eyes to show anger or determination or open them wide to show surprise. Many of today's stock manga and anime facial expressions originated as limited animation techniques.

Japanese animators came up with other ways to use the camera to save animation expense. Sometimes they would make a large drawing or painting to establish a location. Instead of filming thirty-two separate drawings for a four-second sequence, the camera would simply pan across the single image, giving the illusion of movement, even though only one drawing was used. Similarly, the filmmakers could hold the camera on one drawing and film it for several seconds for dramatic effect. They might use the camera's lens to zoom in on a face to emphasize a character's reaction at a dramatic moment. Conversely, the camera could cut from one still drawing to another, giving the illusion of movement. The close-ups, pans, zooms, and quick cuts were all used to enhance the storytelling—and they succeeded. Although originally a cost-saving necessity, these limited animation techniques gave anime a distinctive look and feel. By the 1960s manga and anime had a style all their own.

CHAPTER TWO

The Emergence of a Style

One reason for the popularity of manga and anime is the stylization that the artists employ when drawing the characters, especially their faces. The lines are simple, the proportions of facial features are idealized, and the expressions are somewhat static, changing only slightly to convey what a character is thinking and feeling. In their simplicity, manga and anime faces resemble masks, presenting the characters as universal types, rather than as particular individuals. It is a technique that has been a hallmark of Japanese artwork and drama for centuries.

The power of stylization is something that the Irish poet and playwright William Butler Yeats recognized early in the twentieth century. Yeats criticized the realistic theater that was emerging in the plays of Henrik Ibsen, Anton Chekov, and others as "restless mimicries of the surface of life."[8] He believed that drama should depict a deeper side of human experience. Working from this premise, Yeats created highly stylized plays that featured characters wearing masks, speaking in poetry, and acting out the play's climactic scene in dance. Yeats took no credit for this approach. He said that he was inspired by the Japanese Noh, a type of masked theater that has been performed since the fourteenth century. Noh theater, the later Kabuki theater, and Japanese street puppetry, known as Bunraku, all influenced the development of manga and anime. Like these dramatic forms, manga and anime eschew realistic drawing that mimics exact human features or environmental details to create more universal characters, themes, and stories.

Masks and Anime

The influence of Japanese theater permeates all manga and anime, but it is particularly evident in Hayao Miyazaki's 2001 anime film, *Spirited Away*. The movie tells the story of a ten-year-old girl named Chihiro who enters the realm of the kami, the supernatural beings of the Shinto religion, so she can find a way to undo a spell that has turned her parents into pigs. One of the characters she meets is No-Face, a figure wearing a black shroud and a white mask. "No-Face's neutral mask aesthetically and thematically resembles the masks utilized in Noh theatre," observes theater artist Miranda Barrientos. "Miyazaki uses Noh aesthetics [to] create the personality, or rather lack of personality, of No-Face."[9]

The influence of Japanese Noh theater can be seen in Hayao Miyazaki's 2001 anime film, Spirited Away. In this scene, ten-year-old Chihiro meets No-Face, a figure wearing a black shroud and white mask. The mask is characteristic of Noh theater.

The neutral expression of No-Face's mask is both mysterious and frightening, conveying the fact that the character is a dark spirit that has no personality of its own but instead takes on the personalities of the creatures it devours. The expression is one of about sixty basic types in Noh theater. "Masks play an integral role in characterization," explains Eric C. Rath, a professor of Japanese history at the University of Kansas. "The features of a mask establish the character's gender, age, and social ranking."[10]

The idea of using masks is not to hide a character's personality and emotions but rather to convey the emotions quickly and to allow the audience to participate in the drama by reading the expressions. "Even though the mask covers an actor's facial expressions, the use of the mask in Noh is not an abandonment of facial expressions altogether," writes Illya Szilak, an artist, writer,

Toriyama Explains Goku's Tail

Goku, the hero of Akira Toriyama's fantasy manga *Dragon Ball*, has a tail. In an interview commemorating the thirtieth anniversary of *Dragon Ball*'s debut, Toriyama told the story behind creating Goku's unusual feature.

> I think it boils down to the idea that it's more interesting to have the weak-looking, plain guys be strong. With Goku, he started out just being a straight-up monkey. Then I thought about it some more and made him a human, but [Toriyama's editor] Torishima-*san* said that he needed to have something to set him apart, so I gave him a tail, but it just kept getting in the way. . . .
>
> I'm always thinking about how things are supposed to work, so it was a real pain to figure out how he'd put his pants on or stuff like that. That's what always bugged me most. Is there a hole in the pants? Does he put his tail through first, then put the pants on? So that made me want to just get rid of the darn thing . . . which I did, in the end.

Quoted in Kanzenshuu, "Akira Toriyama Interview: *Dragon Ball* and Akira Toriyama," January 21, 2016. www.kanzenshuu.com.

and theater director. "Rather, its intent is to stylize and codify the facial expressions through the use of the mask and to stimulate the imagination of the audience."[11]

Stock Expressions

Manga and anime artists also use stylized faces to convey a character's personality and emotions. They draw the characters' heads and faces larger than they would be in real life, making it easier for the audience to read the characters' expressions. The artists also make the eyes, which are the focal point for conveying emotion, disproportionately large. The nose and chin are small, making the eyes appear even larger by contrast. The petite features also give the characters an idealized, youthful appearance.

Manga and anime artists depict the eyes, eyebrows, and mouth in certain conventional ways to show how the character is feeling. For example, to convey happiness and contentment, the artist will draw the character with a big smile and the eyes closed. To show a character in love, the smile will be smaller, and the eyes will be open, with the pupils larger and containing more reflections than usual. To express surprise, the artist draws the mouth in a circular shape and renders the eyes wide open, with the eyebrows raised. For anger, the artist draws squinting eyes, with the eyebrows angled down and the mouth curved in a slight frown. To illustrate plotting or scheming, the artist draws the eyes squinting as in anger but with the mouth drawn up in an evil smile. Fright, embarrassment, puzzlement, and other emotions are likewise conveyed through variations in the character's eyes and mouth.

Occasionally, manga and anime artists will use a type of icon to convey emotion. For example, the artist may place a single teardrop on the character's cheek to show sadness, especially if the character is unable or unwilling to cry in a certain situation. Like Noh and Kabuki masks, these expressions have become standardized into basic stock forms. "I don't consider them pictures," Osamu Tezuka, the "Godfather of Manga," once observed. "In reality I'm not drawing. I'm writing a story with a unique type of symbol."[12] Rather than being bored by the stock expressions, readers and moviegoers welcome them as a way to easily understand what the characters are feeling during the often fast-paced action. These easy-to-read expressions are one of the reasons that manga and anime are so popular.

While the facial expressions in manga and anime are similar from character to character, their overall appearances are not. Manga and anime artists use hairstyles, clothing, and eye color to create unique, instantly recognizable characters. Here, again, realism is not a concern. Manga and anime characters can have traditional hair colors of black, brown, yellow, and red, but they can also have blue, green, purple, or any other color of hair. Anything goes!

Like facial expressions, hairstyles have developed into recognizable types. Male main characters often have wild, spiky hair-

Hairstyles are one feature used by anime and manga artists to create unique, instantly recognizable characters. Artists use a range of hair colors and cuts to develop characters' personalities.

Manga and Anime Hairstyles

Manga and anime artists have developed hairstyles that quickly identify character types, emotions, and even superpowers. The website TV Tropes describes some of the popular manga and anime hairstyles.

- Compressed Hair—a large amount of hair is easily compressed into a smaller shape . . .
- Expressive Hair—hair that is independently mobile and responsive to mood. . . .
- Hair Reboot—seemingly destroyed hair can be returned to its proper shape and volume by merely shaking it
- Hair Wings—hair that doubles as wings . . .
- Hammerspace Hair—a character pulls out something they were storing in their hair
- Helicopter Hair—hair that works as a propeller, lifting the character into the air . . .
- Idiot Hair—a single strand of hair that constantly sticks up, usually to indicate low intelligence . . .
- Motherly Side Plait—hair braided loosely and resting on the shoulder indicates motherhood . . .
- Peek-a-Bangs—hair that covers one eye
- Prehensile Hair—tentacle-like hair . . .
- Slipknot Ponytail—hair that falls loose during fights
- World of Technicolor Hair—everyone has an unnatural hair color and it is not treated as odd

TV Tropes, "Anime Hair." https://tvtropes.org.

styles to set them apart from other characters. These outlandish hairstyles make the heroes identifiable even when shown in silhouette. Longish hair on a male character often denotes a "pretty boy" personality. Long sideburns are shorthand for a hot-blooded young man. To portray an upper-class woman, the artist might give the character a "*hime* cut," with long hair in the back, bangs in front, and sidelocks framing the face. A variation of this style features ringlets on each side of the face that hang in front of the shoulders, identifying the character as an *ojou*—a high-class, wealthy young woman. Female action characters often wear their hair in braids to keep their tresses out of their face when fighting.

Supernatural Sagas

Manga and anime artists have also borrowed other conventions from Noh and Kabuki theater. For example, in *Spirited Away*, No-Face is mostly silent, like many of the actors in Noh theater. Significantly, Chihiro first sees No-Face when she crosses a bridge leading to a bathhouse. Classic Noh theaters include a bridge on the right side of the stage that symbolizes a passageway that connects the earthly and spiritual realms. When Chihiro crosses the bridge, she also enters a spiritual realm.

As in Japanese scrolls, Noh theater, and street puppetry, manga and anime artists often tell the stories of legendary heroes who encounter and sometimes battle supernatural beings. Such was the case in Miyazaki's 1997 anime film, *Princess Mononoke*, in which the main character, Ashitaka, battles and defeats a demon, but not before it wounds him and curses him. Like *Spirited Away*, *Princess Mononoke* includes various supernatural beings from Japanese folklore.

In addition to Miyazaki, many other manga and anime artists also depict clashes between figures from different spiritual realms. For example, the popular manga and anime series *GeGeGe no Kitarō*, created by Shigeru Mizuki, follows the adventures of a young hero named Kitarō, who is a supernatural being from Japanese folklore known as a *yōkai*. Throughout the series, Kitarō tries to bring peace between humans and other supernatural beings.

Similarly, Akira Toriyama based his highly popular *Dragon Ball* series in part on the sixteenth-century Chinese novel *Journey to the West*. In that story, the main character, Tang Sanzang, encounters various demons and animal spirits. Toriyama was also inspired by the nineteenth-century Japanese novel *The Chronicles of the Eight Dog Heroes of the Satomi Clan of Nanso*, a tale with spiritual themes. It tells the story of a character named Daisuke, who takes the form of a Buddhist priest and sets out to collect eight sacred prayer beads. Toriyama's story also includes supernatural elements. It centers on a monkey-tailed boy named Goku who helps a teenage girl named Bulma in her quest to collect seven balls that can be used to summon a wish-granting dragon.

The clash between humans and supernatural beings is a theme borrowed from classic Japanese theater and literature, but it is not limited to stories about the past. For example, Noriaki "Tite" Kubo's popular manga series *Bleach* has a contemporary urban setting. In it, the main character, Ichigo Kurosaki, is an ordinary high school student except for the fact that he can see

The clash between humans and supernatural beings is a theme borrowed from classic Japanese theater and literature. In Bleach, Ichigo Kurosaki gains special powers for battling evil when he dons a half mask (similar to this one).

and hear ghosts. Ichigo eventually encounters Rukia Kuchiki, a kami that is required to destroy evil spirits and send good spirits to the afterlife. When Rukia is injured, she gives Ichigo a potion that enables him to take her place as a Soul Reaper, bringing him into conflict with many other spirits and forming the basis of the series' plotlines.

The fantasy element of many manga and anime series sets them apart from Western superhero stories, including those featuring Batman, Superman, Spider-Man, the Justice League, and many more. Typically, the Western stories are set in contemporary times and involve struggles between the heroes and villains who are out for worldly gains—money, power, or both. Western superheroes are usually defending earthly values, including law and order, justice, and public safety.

Sometimes Western comics and animated movies explore psychological struggles, but rarely if ever do they concern themselves with spiritual matters. This stands in contrast to many manga and anime series, especially those based on traditional Japanese folklore and drama, which often reflect Buddhist or Shinto spiritual concerns. Such works often "celebrate deities, poetry, longevity, fertility, or harmony; or exorcize external or internal ghosts and demons,"[13] writes Karen Brazell, a translator of Japanese literature. These timeless, transcendent themes give manga and anime a universality that connects with audiences around the world, making the Japanese art form a global phenomenon.

CHAPTER THREE

Rise of the Giant Robots

A hunger for escapist entertainment fueled the rise of manga and anime in postwar Japan. New manga publishers sprang up to cash in on the craze, and many young artists traveled to Tokyo to try to make a career as a mangaka. Japanese film companies also wanted in on the action. They paid the manga artists to adapt their work to films and television shows. While manga and anime skyrocketed in popularity within Japan, it would take years for the Japanese art forms to make an impact outside the country.

The most prominent of the new mangaka was Osamu Tezuka, who was born November 3, 1928, in Osaka, Japan. Tezuka sold his first manga, a four-panel cartoon strip entitled *Diary of Mā-chan*, about a mischievous boy named Mā-chan, in 1946, when Tezuka was only seventeen years old. The cartoon was a hit, and a toy company even brought out a doll based on the popular character. Encouraged by this success, Tezuka traveled to Tokyo to pitch a single manga story, known as a one-shot, to the magazine *Hello Manga*. The editor he met there, Shichima Sakai, not only accepted Tezuka's one-shot but offered to team up with him to do a new manga series based on Robert Louis Stevenson's 1883 novel *Treasure Island*. Serialized in 1947, *Shin Takara-jima* (*New Treasure Island*) was a huge success, with the episodes collected into a *tankōbon*, or manga book, that sold an astounding four hundred thousand copies.

TREASURE ISLAND

BY

ROBERT LOUIS STEVENSON

By late 1950, just four years after starting his career as a mangaka, Tezuka had published twenty-six different one-shot mangas and four manga series. None of his series lasted more than a few months, but his fifth series, *Janguru Taitei* (*Jungle Emperor*), the story of a lion cub named Leo, would run from 1950 to 1954 and eventually be made into a popular anime film, known in the West as *Kimba the White Lion*.

An Amiable Automaton

While *Jungle Emperor* was beginning to gain a following, Tezuka had an idea that would launch his career into the stratosphere and change manga and anime forever. He imagined a childlike robot that would struggle against all odds to broker peace between humans and an invading force of millions of aliens whose planet had been destroyed by an explosion thousands of years before. He named the series after his peacekeeping robot, *Ambassador Atom*. Children loved Ambassador Atom, which looked and behaved like a naive schoolboy but had the intelligence of a supercomputer.

Ambassador Atom proved so popular that when the series ended after eleven months, in March 1952, Tezuka's editor, Takeshi Kanai, asked the young artist to build a new series around his popular character. Tezuka doubted whether his young robot could sustain another series. "At first he was completely doll-like," Tezuka later said. "He had no personality, no feelings, and he acted as a silly robot foil for the other characters in the story."[14] Kanai understood Tezuka's concerns, but he offered a suggestion. "Make him a robot with a human personality," Kanai said. "Instead of making him a character that takes off his head and arms for a gag, make him a robot with emotions, who laughs, cries, and gets angry when he senses injustice."[15]

Tezuka took Kanai's advice, and the new series, *Mighty Atom*, debuted later in 1952. The new, more human robot, Atom, was even more popular than the original. A growing legion of fans kept the manga series going for the next sixteen years.

Conquering the Small Screen

In 1961 Tezuka made a fateful decision. After the animation studio Tōei Dōga had successfully adapted his popular manga story *Boku no Songokū* (*My Monkey King*) as an animated feature film, Tezuka decided to found his own animation studio, Mushi Production. The studio's first move was to animate Tezuka's most popular character, Atom. After seeing a ten-minute pilot featuring the childlike robot, Fuji TV executives agreed to air the series.

With a fan base from the manga series numbering in the millions, the *Mighty Atom* television series was a hit from its first airing on January 1, 1963. Twenty-seven percent of Japanese television viewers at that time slot tuned in to watch the first episode, "The Birth of Mighty Atom." The lovable little android with big eyes and spiky hair became a cultural phenomenon. The eighty-fourth episode, "Dolphin Civilization," broadcast on August 29, 1964, set a ratings record that still stands. That night, 40 percent of all Japanese television viewers were watching *Mighty Atom*.

Impressed by *Mighty Atom*'s success in Japan, Fred Ladd, a producer for the American television network NBC, acquired the rights to broadcast the program in the United States. Ladd hired English-speaking actors to voice the various parts, a practice known as dubbing, and added the show to NBC's Saturday morning cartoon lineup. To avoid the negative connotations of the word *atom* arising from the use of the atom bomb against Japan in World War II, and because the main character could fly using rocket engines in his legs, NBC renamed the series *Astro Boy*. Debuting on September 7, 1963, *Astro Boy* was the first Japanese animation series to be shown to US viewers. Millions of American children were charmed by the boyish robot, and NBC ended up broadcasting 104 episodes from 1963 to 1966. Without the built-in fan base from the manga series, *Astro Boy* was not the ratings powerhouse it had been in Japan, but the program's modest success convinced Ladd to keep an eye on Japanese anime for future projects.

Astro Boy debuted in the United States in 1963. It was the first Japanese animation series to be shown to US viewers, who were charmed by the flying boyish robot.

A Massive Star

It did not take long for Ladd to find his next anime success. Later in 1963 Ladd saw drawings from Mitsuteru Yokoyama's manga and animated series *Tetsujin-28* (*Iron Man Number 28*), featuring a gigantic robot that was remote-controlled by a tech-savvy twelve-year-old boy named Jimmy Sparks. Like *Astro Boy*, the outsized automaton battled villains, but *Tetsujin-28*'s clashes were more violent and exciting than those of *Astro Boy*.

Ladd formed his own production company to bring *Tetsujin-28* to the small screen. Since the name Iron Man was already associated with a Marvel Comics hero, Ladd christened his massive protagonist Gigantor and named the series after it. *Gigantor* was an immediate hit with action-hungry American youths. Critics found *Gigantor*'s characters one dimensional, and many parents condemned the series as too violent, but kids loved the idea that a youngster could deftly control a mechanical colossus to overpower dangerous villains, succeeding where the adults around them could not. It was a story line that would be repeated with increasing success over the next sixty years. It was also a scenario that future generations of youngsters would experience for themselves as they used handheld devices similar to the one used by Jimmy Sparks to control robots and other powerful characters in video and virtual reality games.

Controlling a Monster

One of the fans of *Gigantor* was a mangaka named Kiyoshi Nagai, known by his pen name Go Nagai. The successful creator of a manga series about supernatural beings, Nagai was fascinated by the idea of basing a new series on robots. Try as he might to create something original, Nagai felt that all his robot concepts were too similar to *Gigantor* and *Astro Boy*. But Nagai's imagination never rested. One day, watching drivers trapped in a massive traffic jam, the artist had an intriguing thought: "If a car had arms and legs, then there would be no problems like this!"[16] He imagined a giant robot, several stories high, that could just step over the traffic. Inside, at the controls, would be a human pilot. Nagai called his creation Mazinger Z.

The idea of a human being teaming up with an oversized robot was similar to *Gigantor*, but instead of controlling the mechanized behemoth from afar, Mazinger Z's pilot would be embedded inside. That made it different enough to satisfy Nagai's quest for originality. He also thought the idea would appeal to young readers. "Kids want to turn into adults fast," says Nagai. "I just wanted to take that feeling and turn it into a human riding inside a robot."[17] Originally, Nagai pictured a motorcyclist racing up the robot's back and docking inside its head. However, because of the success of an animated television series featuring a motorcycle-riding superhero named Kamen Rider, Nagai switched the pilot's vehicle to a futuristic hovercraft.

Tezuka Speaks to Future Generations

Osamu Tezuka spent a lot of time thinking about the future. He put down some of his thoughts in a book entitled *Save Our Mother Earth: To the Youth of the 21st Century*. Passages from the book are excerpted here.

Our beautiful glass-like earth, so easily shattered, floats in the loneliness of the vast universe. Against the unending blackness of the depths of the universe, how beautiful this planet of water is: perhaps it represents the world of mysticism itself. If just once we could be witness to that vast universe, it may be that we would never want to harm our precious air, water, greenery, or our oceans again. . . .

No matter how far mankind goes in terms of the material civilization, the fact remains that he is a part of the natural world, and no matter how much science progresses, the power of nature cannot be denied. Indeed, by rejecting nature, we reject our own humanity. . . .

We humans have relentlessly pursued material happiness in pursuit of our needs, without any hesitation whatsoever. Now may be our last chance to stop, take a look around, and think about what we are doing.

Osamu Tezuka, "Message for Earth," Tezuka Osamu Official Website, 2021. https://tezuka osamu.net.

Another feature Nagai borrowed from *Gigantor* was the idea of having a young person be the hero of the manga. Nagai made the robot's pilot a seventeen-year-old high school student named Koji Kabuto. "What I had in common with the children that were seeing robots was that I wanted to have this incredible power," says Nagai. "I wanted to give a teenaged character a suit of armor that would turn him into a hero."[18]

Honoring Ancestors

Nagai realized that a teenager would not have the time, resources, or know-how to build a sophisticated machine. For the sake of plausibility, Nagai did not make Koji the creator of Mazinger Z. Instead, he had the teenager inherit Mazinger Z from his late grandfather, Juzo Kabuto, a brilliant professor who had created the gargantuan robot to battle an army of mechanized warriors commanded by the evil Dr. Hell. Professor Kabuto formed the robot out of an ultrastrong metal known as Super Alloy Z, which was derived from the fictional element Japanium, which can only be found near Mount Fuji. In addition to believability, the intergenerational story line reflects Shinto beliefs about the connection people have to their deceased ancestors.

Debuting in the manga magazine *Weekly Shōnen Jump* in October 1972, *Mazinger Z* was an instant hit. Within two months Fuji TV had developed an anime television series featuring the towering titan and his youthful pilot. The television version ran for ninety-two episodes, from December 1972 to September 1974. The series was a ratings success, reaching a 30 percent share of the viewing audience in March 1974. Its popularity spawned a second manga series and various branded merchandise, including die-cast metal toys and the first of the Bandai Company's Jumbo Machinder line of plastic action toys, which stand about 24 inches (61 cm) high. Released in 1973, the Jumbo Machinder Mazinger Z sold more than four hundred thousand units in its first five months.

Go Nagai's idea for an enormous robot piloted by a person immediately caught on in its 1972 manga debut. Mazinger Z was soon transformed into anime and spawned dozens of other manga and anime featuring giant robots piloted by young heroes.

Even as the *Mazinger Z* anime series was running, Nagai was planning a sequel entitled *Great Mazinger*. At the end of the original series, Mazinger Z is destroyed, but Koji is saved by a new super robot, Great Mazinger. The new robot is piloted by a young man named Tetsuya Tsurugi, an orphan who was raised and trained by Koji's father, Kenzo Kabuto. Kenzo also developed a stronger Japanium alloy to make the new, more powerful robot. Again, the intergenerational story line—especially the refinement of Professor Kabuto's creations by his son Kenzo—reflects the Shinto values of reverence and devotion toward one's ancestors.

Great Mazinger was another ratings hit for Nagai and Fuji TV. Although the sequel did not quite soar to the heights of its predecessor, it was popular enough to last for fifty-six episodes from 1974 to 1975. Nagai also developed three anime films featuring the original Mazinger Z. In one, Mazinger Z vs. Devilman (1973), the massive robot clashes with the villain from Nagai's supernatural manga series Devilman. In another, Mazinger Z vs. Dr. Hell (1973), the teenager and his massive fighting machine face off with Professor Kabuto's nemesis, Dr. Hell. The third sequel, Mazinger Z vs. the Great General of Darkness (1974), serves as a bridge between the two television series, Mazinger Z and Great Mazinger. In one scene, while the badly damaged Mazinger Z is being repaired, Koji is shown looking at pictures of his father and grandfather and thinking about his future—another intergenerational scene that resonates with Shintoism.

A Quest for Originality

A successful mangaka in the realm of supernatural fantasy, Go Nagai wanted to try his hand at creating a robot series. Nagai's personal and professional standards drove him to create something original and not just copy the robot series he admired, Astro Boy and Gigantor. New ideas are hard to find, however. Eventually, Nagai hit upon the idea of having a human being control a giant robot from a cockpit located in the massive machine's head. Nagai was pleased with his creative breakthrough, and he used it to develop Mazinger Z. But Nagai's idea was not quite as original as it seemed. Another manga series, Demon Lord Dante, featured a giant demon that had killed a student named Ryo Utsugi and absorbed his soul. Because Utsugi's spirit merged with that of the demon, the young man's head was embedded in the demon's forehead, where it could watch and influence the demon's actions, just like the driver of Mazinger Z. Nagai was not worried about the creator of Demon Lord Dante suing him or criticizing him for copying his idea, however. That is because he was the creator of Demon Lord Dante. In his quest for originality, Nagai had copied himself.

Going Global

In 1977 Toei Animation obtained the rights to dub thirty episodes of *Mazinger Z* into English. The series aired in Hawaii and the Philippines, where the national language is Tagalog, but students learn English as well. The show was such a hit in the Philippines that Toei commissioned the dubbing of additional episodes for the local market. The Toei adaptations were not shown in the rest of the United States, but in the 1980s Three B. Productions, a US production company, adapted *Mazinger Z* for American audiences. Unlike the Toei production, which retained the character names and plotlines of the original series, the Three B. version edited the story line and changed the name of the characters. Renamed *Tranzor Z*, the English-dubbed program debuted in 1985 and ran for sixty-five episodes.

> "In creating *Mazinger Z* and kicking off the super robot revolution, Go Nagai discovered a resilient formula, one almost as strong as Alloy Z itself."[19]
>
> —Michael Toole, television critic

When Cartoon Network went on the air in 1992, it added *Tranzor Z* to its lineup, introducing a whole new generation to the titanic robot and its teenage pilot. This was the series that brought anime to the attention of the English-speaking world. The series and its sequels also spawned dozens of other manga and anime featuring giant robots piloted by young heroes riding in their cockpits—a category of manga and anime called "mecha," short for "mechanical." Like *Mazinger Z*, these mecha series appeal to the youthful craving for independence and respect in the adult world. "In creating *Mazinger Z* and kicking off the super robot revolution, Go Nagai discovered a resilient formula," observes television critic Michael Toole, "one almost as strong as Alloy Z itself."[19]

CHAPTER FOUR

Big Screen Success

When anime first showed up in the United States, entertainment executives thought of it as something for television, if they thought of it at all. In Japan, however, anime films were becoming a big part of the entertainment market. In 1958 Toei Animation released Japan's first color anime feature film, *Hakujaden* (*The Tale of the White Serpent*), a story based on a Chinese folktale, to critical and box office success. The next year, the studio released *Shōnen Sarutobi Sasuke* (*Young Sarutobi Sasuke*) to further acclaim. Throughout the 1960s Toei released at least one animated feature film a year—moneymakers all.

In 1961 American film studio MGM decided to release three anime films in the United States. The studio dubbed the dialogue into English and retitled the movies to appeal to American audiences. *Hakujaden* became *Panda and the Magic Serpent*, *Shōnen Sarutobi Sasuke* became *Magic Boy*, and *Saiyūki* (*Journey to the West*) became *Alakazam the Great*. American critics generally praised the films, and a small number of moviegoers enjoyed the exotic stories, characters, and artwork. But the public at large ignored the movies.

Throughout the 1960s various American film studios continued releasing anime films in hopes of making a quick profit. The films were available from the Japanese filmmakers for small fees, and dubbing and editing the movies was cheap. The movies generally made money, but none became box office hits. By the 1980s, however, a growing

During the 1960s, a growing number of American children and teens were becoming fans of anime on television. The auto racing series Speed Racer (pictured) was among the series that appealed to American youth.

number of American children and teens were becoming fans of anime on television, especially *Tranzor Z*, the auto racing series *Speed Racer*, and *Marine Boy*, the story of Marine, a genetically altered boy with superhuman swimming ability, and Splasher, his pet white dolphin.

Show Business

The first anime film to make a big impact in the United States was not solely a Japanese film. It was a collaboration between US and Japanese studios. And its premise did not emerge from the mind of a mangaka or an anime screenwriter. It arose in the headquarters of America's largest toy maker, Hasbro. The company had just concluded a deal with Japanese toy maker Takara to manufacture small toys that cleverly changed from everyday objects, such as cars, into humanoid robots. Hasbro called the new toy line Transformers. Inspired by the company's successful collaboration with Marvel Comics to create an animated series around its military action figure, G.I. Joe, Hasbro approached Marvel with the idea of developing a new animated series around the shape-shifting robots.

Merchandise tie-ins with movies were nothing new. Hollywood had been licensing toys and dolls based on films ever since Walt Disney's Mickey Mouse whistled his way down the Mississippi in 1928's *Steamboat Willie*. The Walt Disney Company has made a fortune by selling everything from snow globes to Halloween costumes based on its animated movies. But like a robot turning back into a car, *The Transformers* reversed the process. The toys came first, and the television series, comic books, and movies followed.

Jim Shooter, Marvel's editor in chief, came up with the basic story line for *The Transformers*: two factions of giant alien robots—the Autobots and the Decepticons—crash-land on Earth and remain buried for 4 million years. When they awaken in 1984, the Decepticons begin plundering Earth for energy resources. The Autobots attempt to stop them. Unlike the mecha robots of Japanese anime, the Transformers do not have human pilots. Instead, they possess a kind of soul that gives them intelligence, autonomy, and the ability to choose between good and evil.

Moving to the Big Screen

When it came time to animate the series, Hasbro turned to the masters of mecha—Toei Animation in Japan. Although American in concept, *The Transformers* was anime from top to bottom. Fueled by the synergy with Hasbro's innovative toy line, the weekly series was a ratings winner. Within two years, Hasbro decided to take its metamorphosing machines to the big screen. The producers cast several leading actors for the voice roles, including Judd Nelson, Robert Stack, Leonard Nimoy, and Orson Welles in his final role.

Despite the strong cast, most movie critics panned the movie when it was released in 1986. "I am offended that *The Transformers* is a 90-minute toy commercial," wrote Scott Cain of the *Atlanta Constitution*. "Even worse, it paints a future in which war is incessant."[20] Jack Zink of the *South Florida Sun Sentinel* called it "a wall-to-wall demolition derby for kids" with a "maddeningly simple story."[21]

Although it only made $5.8 million at the US box office, *The Transformers* was still the top-grossing anime film in the United States to that point. The film brought in additional revenue from its release in eight other countries worldwide, including the United Kingdom, Australia, Brazil, France, and Japan. When the movie was released on video in 1987, it remained in the top twenty-five of *Billboard*'s Top Kid Video Sales chart for at least forty weeks. It was enough of a success to have American film studios and distributors on the lookout for other animated gems from Japan.

A Rising Star

American film distributors did not have to wait long to find a rising star. A manga artist and movie director named Hayao Miyazaki had been making a name for himself in Japan with a series of visually stunning and thematically rich anime films. His 1979 film *The Castle of Cagliostro* received the Ōfuji Noburō Award for an outstanding animated movie at the prestigious Mainichi Film Awards, sponsored by *Mainichi Shinbun*, a leading Japanese newspaper. His 1984 film, *Nausicaä of the Valley of the Wind*, was another critical success and, unlike *The Castle of Cagliostro*, a box office success as well, earning about $14 million in Japanese theaters. Based on Miyazaki's popular manga series, the movie tells the story of Nausicaä, a young princess who lives one thousand years in the future, after a cataclysmic war has wiped out human civilization and despoiled the planet. Young as she is, Nausicaä drives invaders from her valley home and begins the process of restoring the toxic water and soil with purifying plants. In 2009 the Japanese film magazine *Kinema Junpo* named *Nausicaä of the Valley of the Wind* the second-greatest Japanese animated film of all time.

Miyazaki's growing popularity attracted the attention of Japan Airlines, which ordered an English dub of the forty-seven-year-old director's 1988 fantasy film, *My Neighbor Totoro*, to be shown on its transpacific flights. In the film, a girl named Mei befriends a large forest spirit she calls Totoro outside the rural home where her mother is recuperating from an illness. The film's depiction of spiritualism and harmony with nature made it an ideal introduction to Japanese culture, the Japan Airlines executives believed. The in-flight movie was the first time many Westerners had seen Miyazaki's work. The film won several awards, including the Animage Anime Grand Prix and the Kinema Junpo Award for Best Film of 1988.

Changing Views on *The Transformers*

When *The Transformers* arrived in US theaters in 1986, many critics objected to the movie's commercialism. Some saw the film as nothing more than an eighty-five-minute promo for Hasbro's new line of toy robots. More than thirty years later, film critic Ryan Lambie sees it differently.

> In retrospect, Hasbro's cold business decision—to wipe out one generation of toys in order to replace them with new ones—resulted in a far more effective movie. . . . *Transformers: The Movie* wound up being a story about death, transfiguration, guilt and redemption. It's a coming-of-age story about a young and reckless Autobot . . . growing into the role of a heroic leader. . . .
>
> It's as though Hasbro, once it was satisfied that the film would involve killing lots of Transformers and introduce new ones, simply left the filmmakers to their own devices. . . .
>
> It's full of quirky ideas that were placed there simply because its writers and artists felt like throwing them in. It's those quirks . . . that have seen the 1986 movie endure over the past 30 years. Full of color and rich with detail, [it] is a sublime time capsule from a decade of excess.

Ryan Lambie, "The Quirky Brilliance of *Transformers: The Movie*," Den of Geek, December 20, 2018. www.denofgeek.com.

Encouraged by the positive reaction to *My Neighbor Totoro*, Japan Airlines hired Miyazaki to adapt his successful manga *The Age of the Flying Boat*, the story of a retired Italian Air Force pilot whose head has been changed by a curse into that of a pig, into another in-flight movie. First appearing on Japan Airlines flights, *Porco Rosso* (Italian for "Red Pig") debuted in Japanese theaters on July 18, 1992, and immediately rose to number one in box-office receipts. It ended the year as the top-grossing film of the year in Japan, hauling in $43 million. The whimsical cartoon adventure was a hit with the critics as well, not only in Japan but around the world. It was named the best feature-length film of the year at the 1993 Annecy International Animated Film Festival in Annecy, France, soaring over entries from around the world. Anime had become a force in the motion picture industry.

In the 1988 fantasy film My Neighbor Totoro *a young girl befriends a large forest spirit she calls Totoro. The film's depiction of spiritualism and harmony with nature made it an ideal introduction to Japanese culture for US viewers.*

Creative Powerhouse

Miyazaki led anime to new heights, but he was not alone in his efforts. In June 1985 Miyazaki teamed up with film director Isao Takahata, who had collaborated with Miyazaki on television and movie projects for twenty years, and movie producer Toshio Suzuki, who had also worked on *Nausicaä*, to found their own animation company, Studio Ghibli. By 1995 Miyazaki had written and directed four films for the fledgling studio, and Takahata had written and directed three: *Grave of the Fireflies*, *Only Yesterday*, and *Pom Poko*. The studio had also produced two other films—*Ocean Waves* and *Whisper of the Heart*—by other screenwriters.

Walt Disney Studios, which had led the animation industry for fifty years, took notice of the upstart Japanese studio. In 1996 Disney acquired worldwide distribution rights to the Studio Ghibli library. It used top-flight actors to redub all previously dubbed films into various languages while honoring Miyazaki's demand that none of the studio's films be cut or edited without permission. One by one, Disney released the Studio Ghibli works on DVD, bringing the work of Miyazaki and Takahata into millions of homes around the world. Disney also began to release the newly dubbed films into theaters, starting in 1998 with *Kiki's Delivery Service*, Miyazaki's 1989 film about a young witch trying to make her way in the world by using her flying broomstick to deliver baked goods. Under the joint venture, Disney dubbed and released Studio Ghibli's new movies as well, including Miyazaki's *Princess Mononoke* (1997), *Spirited Away* (2001), *Howl's Moving Castle* (2004), and *Ponyo* (2008).

Two Studio Ghibli films set all-time Japanese box office records, not just for animated films but for all films. In 1997 *Princess Mononoke* surpassed the American science fiction movie *E.T.: The Extra-Terrestrial* to become the highest-grossing film in Japan's history. That record was broken by *Titanic* a few months later. But in 2001, *Spirited Away* shattered *Titanic*'s record, earning $224 million in Japan alone.

A Japanese Gold Rush

Noting Disney's tie-up with Studio Ghibli and sensing the dawn of a new era in animation, other US distributors began to look toward Japan to cash in on the anime craze. Since Disney and Studio Ghibli closed their deal in 1997, more than 175 feature-length anime films have been released in theaters in the United States, including twenty-one by animation giant Toei. Some of these were megahits.

In 1999 Warner Brothers distributed *Pokémon: The First Movie*, the first of nine movies produced by animation studio OLM. *Pokémon: The First Movie* followed the blueprint of the *Transformers* movies, growing out of and complementing a popular line of trading cards, toys, video games, and TV shows. With a built-in audience of trading card fans and boosted by a promotional tie-in with Burger King, *Pokémon: The First Movie* was the first anime film to top the US box office, debuting at number one on November 10, 1999. Critics, however, were not impressed. "The story is idiotic," wrote Roger Ebert of the *Chicago Sun-Times*. "I can't recommend the film or work up much enthusiasm for it because there is no level at which it enriches a young viewer, by encouraging thinking or observation. It's just a sound-and-light show, linked to the marketing push for Pokemon in general."[22] Despite the thumbs-down from Ebert and others, the film earned $85.7 million by the time its first run ended in February 2000.

> "I can't recommend [*Pokémon: The First Movie*] or work up much enthusiasm for it because there is no level at which it enriches a young viewer, by encouraging thinking or observation."[22]
>
> —Roger Ebert, film critic for the *Chicago Sun-Times*

Two more *Pokémon* movies followed, and while not as popular as the first installment, they both did well. With US gross receipts exceeding $17 million, *Pokémon 3 the Movie: Spell of the Unown* was the ninth-highest-grossing anime film in the US market as of 2023. Films based on the Digimon and Yu-Gi-Oh! toy and video franchises also scored box office successes. As of 2023, *Yu-Gi-Oh! The*

An Artistic and Commercial Success

Rarely are blockbuster movies artistic triumphs, or artistic triumphs blockbuster movies. *Spirited Away* is both. It earned $395.8 million at the box office, and it received twenty-three major film awards, including Best Animated Feature at the 75th Academy Awards ceremony. In 2017 the *New York Times* ranked *Spirited Away* number two on its list of "The 25 Best Films of the 21st Century So Far." Director Guillermo del Toro, best known for his Academy Award–winning fantasy horror film *Pan's Labyrinth*, writes:

> In "Spirited Away" you have a girl right at the threshold of becoming a young woman and leaving her childhood behind, figuratively and literally. . . . She evolves from her poise, dress, attitude, emotion and spirituality from being a child to being a young woman and coming into her own, and in that position she has to go through the loss of everything. . . . There's a beautiful, very melancholic meditation – the same melancholy that permeates all Miyazaki's films. . . .
>
> There is a moment in which beauty moves you in a way that is impossible to describe. It's not that it's a fabrication, it's that it's an artistic act and you know nothing you will encounter in the natural world will be that pure. Miyazaki has that power.

Quoted in Manohla Dargis and A.O. Scott, "The 25 Best Films of the 21st Century So Far," *New York Times*, June 9, 2017. www.nytimes.com.

Movie—Pyramid of Light (2004) was the seventh-highest-grossing anime film in the US market.

Anime powerhouse Toei has put together a string of hits based on Akira Toriyama's popular *Dragon Ball* manga series, which has sold more than 300 million manga collections worldwide. Although Toei released the first *Dragon Ball* movie in 1986, it took twenty years before a *Dragon Ball* feature was released in the United States, with the double bill of *Dragon Ball Z: Fusion Reborn* and *Dragon Ball Z: The Return of Cooler* debuting in 2006. Since then, seven more *Dragon Ball* movies have been shown in the United States. *Dragon Ball Super: Broly* (2019) ranks as the fourth-highest-grossing anime film in the United States, with $30.7 million in receipts. *Dragon Ball Super: Super Hero* (2022) is not far behind, ranking as the sixth-highest-grossing anime movie in the United States, with receipts of $22.6 million. *Super Hero* was a hit with critics, too. "*Dragon Ball Super: Super Hero* mixes the best of everything there is to love about this fabled franchise," writes film critic Adrian Ruiz. "There are jokes, there are fight scenes, and most importantly, there are character moments that will make you remember why *Dragon Ball* is the Godfather of anime in the west."[23]

Unexpected Success

With the popularity of anime growing by the day, the box office successes of the *Pokémon* and *Dragon Ball* movies were not exactly surprises. But no one was prepared for what happened in 2020, when Japanese animation studio Ufotable released *Demon Slayer: Kimetsu no Yaiba—the Movie: Mugen Train*, the first movie based on Koyoharu Gotouge's dark manga series *Demon Slayer: Kimetsu no Yaiba* (*Blade of Demon Destruction*). Set in the Taishō era of Japan (1912–1926), the manga follows the exploits of Tanjiro Kamado, a boy whose parents were killed and whose sister was turned into a demon in an attack by an evil spirit. Hoping to avenge the killings and save his sister, who retains some human traits, Tanjiro joins a secret society, the Demon Slayers, who have perfected the art of killing the evil spirits.

Preceded by a single twenty-six-episode season of an animated television series based on the manga, *Demon Slayer: Kimetsu no Yaiba—the Movie: Mugen Train* set records even before it opened, with advance ticket receipts in September and October 2020 topping all previous advance sales. When the film debuted on October 16, 2020, it set an opening-day box office record in Japan, grossing $44 million. In January 2021 it became the all-time top-grossing movie in Japan, surpassing the record set nineteen years before by *Spirited Away*.

> "*Dragon Ball Super: Super Hero* mixes the best of everything there is to love about this fabled franchise. There are jokes, there are fight scenes, and most importantly, there are character moments that will make you remember why *Dragon Ball* is the Godfather of anime in the west."[23]
>
> —Adrian Ruiz, film critic

Demon Slayer: Kimetsu no Yaiba—The Movie: Mugen Train *set sales records even before it opened in theaters in 2020. The film is based on Koyoharu Gotouge's dark manga series, which also became a televised anime series.*

Opening in the United States in April 2021, *Demon Slayer: Kimetsu no Yaiba—the Movie: Mugen Train* grossed $21 million in its opening weekend, second to the *Mortal Kombat* reboot ($23 million). In a rare occurrence, the anime film became the top-grossing US movie in the second week of its release. The movie went on to earn more than $507 million worldwide, making it the number one box office attraction of 2021. It was the first time in the history of cinema—going all the way back to 1915, when the first records were kept—that the world's top-grossing motion picture did not originate in the United States. Anime had arrived.

CHAPTER FIVE

The Fun of Fandom

By sheer historical coincidence, the age of computing began at about the same time that manga and anime appeared on the scene after World War II. And while manga and anime did not impact the growth of computing, computing had a major impact on the growth of manga and anime. Personal computing, especially networked computing in the form of the internet, has allowed fans of manga and anime to connect in ways never seen in the annals of popular culture. Online bulletin boards, websites, and social media platforms have allowed fans around the world to share their thoughts, feelings, and enthusiasm for manga and anime, creating a large and growing community. This community, in turn, acts as a multiplier for the popularity of manga and anime.

Fan Fiction

One of the ways that fans of manga, a television series, or a movie can express their enthusiasm for a work is to create something of their own using the characters they know and love. A vignette or a story based on copyrighted materials is known as fan fiction. The act of creating fan fiction, interacting with the characters in one's imagination, can enable fans to feel closer to the work they already admire. Millions of manga and anime fans around the world write and often illustrate their own fan fiction.

Creating a work of fan fiction can be a personally satisfying accomplishment, but sometimes the writer may want to share the work with other fans just to see what they think of it. Sometimes fans are inspired by other fan fiction to try it for themselves, and they want to share their work to perhaps inspire others. In the early days of the internet, fan-fiction writers posted their work on electronic bulletin boards or distributed it via email lists. With the advent of more user-friendly websites, sharing fan fiction became easier.

In 1998 computer programmer Xing Li launched a website called FanFiction.net, which allows users to create profiles, post their work, review other fan fiction, and exchange messages. The site organizes works into several categories, including anime/ manga. The ease of use and large number of users made it a magnet for fan fiction, with more than 12 million registered users.

Novelist N.K. Jemisin, the only author to win the Hugo Award for best science-fiction or fantasy novel three years in a row, credits manga and anime fan fiction for fostering her writing ca- reer. A fan of *Dragon Ball Z*, she began writing fan fiction while in graduate school. "I was miserable and lonely. I didn't have a

The FanFiction website allows users to create profiles, post their work, review other fan fiction, and exchange messages. The site organizes works into several categories, including anime and manga.

lot of friends, or stress relief," she recalls. "Around then was when I became internetted, and one of the first communities I discovered was a fan-fic community." She says that fan fiction is a great vehicle for beginning writers, because they do not have to start from scratch. "Fan fiction tends to have a built-in hook because it's written in a world you're a fan of; you're predisposed to like it," she says. The built-in interest draws readers as well. With that head start, writers can focus on developing their own skills. "You have to find a way to make it not just the world that people are tuning in to read, so they are interested in *your* story,"[24] Jemisin says.

Researchers Katie Davis and Cecilia Aragon at the University of Washington have studied fan fiction, analyzing 61.5 billion words of fan-fiction stories and 6 billion words of reviews posted on FanFiction.net. They found that the average age of a fan-fiction author is seventeen. Because the bonds among fans are strong, the feedback fan-fiction authors receive is overwhelmingly positive. Aragon and Davis report that of the forty-five hundred reviews they analyzed, only 1 percent were "non-constructive negative"[25] reviews.

Online Communities

While millions of anime fans write and comment on fan fiction, millions of others just want to discuss their favorite manga and anime artists and works. There are more than sixty manga and anime fan communities online in which fans can meet to talk about their favorite art form. Websites also carry news, interviews with manga and anime artists, and sneak previews of upcoming manga releases, television series, and movies.

The most important manga and anime website in the United States is Crunchyroll. A joint venture between Sony Pictures, Sony Music Entertainment, and Aniplex, Japan's leading anime licensing company, Crunchyroll allows fans to read manga and watch anime online for a subscription fee. The site has more than one thousand anime titles and about thirty thousand television episodes. With its vast library, Crunchyroll is playing a major role in the growing popularity of anime and manga, making it easy for fans and the just curious to explore the world of the Japanese art form. New anime episodes are available just one hour after they are released in Japan. Crunchyroll has many fan features, including news, reviews, and pages where fans can post photos of themselves and others dressed up as manga and anime characters—a practice known as costume play, or cosplay for short.

A Supportive Audience

University of Washington researchers Cecilia Aragon and Katie Davis spent several years studying fan fiction. To their surprise, they found that the most helpful feedback writers received came from their peers, not from more experienced writers.

> We sought to learn what writers, primarily adolescents and young adults, were gaining from their participation in fanfiction communities. We observed multiple instances of individuals stating their overall writing skills had improved due to their involvement in fanfiction and remarking on the value of mentoring in their achievements.

> As we began our research, we expected to find traditional mentoring relationships with experienced authors teaching younger or less experienced writers. Instead, we discovered a phenomenon that went beyond the standard definitions of mentoring. We found that fanfiction authors (often young people) are publishing stories that may be several hundred thousand words in length. . . . Readers are offering encouragement and constructive feedback on stories, which authors use to improve their writing. All of this happens in a predominantly supportive community atmosphere that stands in stark contrast to the negativity and even hate speech found on so many online sites. Authors experience mentorship from the community, grow as writers, gain recognition for their work, and form meaningful connections with other fans.

Cecilia Aragon and Katie Davis, *Writers in the Secret Garden*. Cambridge, MA: MIT Press, 2019, p. 10.

Bonding with a Character

Cosplay is another way for fans of manga and anime to deepen the connection with the work they admire. Cosplay is more than mere dress-up. When fans assume the look of a character, they often take on the character's personality as well. Just as the author of fan fiction will invent fresh dialogue for a well-known manga or anime character, so too will cosplayers improvise speech and actions consistent with the characters they are representing with their costumes. It may start with simply uttering a character's catchphrase when meeting other cosplayers. But as fans confront different real-life situations at the gatherings they attend, they often improvise more speech and actions in character. This creative process can strengthen the fans' appreciation for the characters they love. "Cosplay . . . is a performance art in which participants wear costumes and accessories to represent a specific character

Cosplay is a way for fans of manga and anime to deepen their connection with the work they admire. When fans assume the look of a character, as these Naruto *fans are doing, they often take on the character's personality as well.*

or idea," says the *Anime Costume Blog*. "This adds authenticity to the entire experience."[26] Cosplay can also have psychological benefits. "For some marginalized identities, cosplay can be particularly empowering," explains psychologist Drea Letamendi. "It allows someone to experience and explore the feelings of being in control, actualizing freedom, being heroic, or sensing oneself as physically strong, revered and respected."[27] An eighteen-year-old cosplayer named Moon says that cosplay helped bring him out of his shell. "Cosplay is a method of expression and escapism and a way to be someone else, even just for a few hours," he says. "With cosplay, I feel more confident and comfortable in myself, and it makes me feel like I'm able to do things I'm normally not able to do. It also helps me express myself in ways that I normally struggle to express."[28]

Cosplay started in Japan in the early 1990s among attendees at manga- and anime-related events, including conventions. It has become popular among attendees at conventions in the United States as well. "Over the last five years, cosplay culture has exploded dramatically, and I'm amazed by the number of attendees who dress up," says Joe Boudrie, director of programming for Phoenix Comicon. "The explosion of pop culture and costuming have created a feedback where each side is making the other grow."[29]

In-Person Gatherings

Conventions and expos also feed the popularity of manga and anime. Except for the last three weeks of December, there is an anime fan expo or film festival every week of the year in different cities across the United States. Most expos include vendors, performance, gaming, and Japanese culture and food. The larger expos feature celebrities from anime film and television. Some offer sketch duels in which manga artists compete at drawing a random character in a particular state or performing an action chosen by the audience. The artists generally have fifteen minutes to complete their drawings, and the winner is determined by the audience. The drawings are typically awarded to members of the audience through a random drawing.

When not attending conventions or expos, manga and anime fans often show their enthusiasm for their favorite art form by incorporating licensed merchandise into their lives. They may wear T-shirts emblazoned with scenes from manga and anime works or carry purses with likenesses of their favorite characters. Dolls, key chains, water bottles—manga and anime decorations can be found everywhere. Some people even cover their cars with over-

Practical Benefits of Cosplay

Cosplay enthusiast Emily Joice writes a blog full of advice for cosplayers. In the excerpt below, Joice describes some of the practical skills that she has learned from cosplay.

- Problem-solving. Every time you create a new costume, you will run into something you have never done before. . . . Every time you run into a new task or unexpected problem, you are forced to use your resources to figure out how to solve it. Overall, it keeps your brain flexible so you can get good at approaching problems from different perspectives.

- Communication. Not only will you need to learn social skills while cosplaying at conventions, but good communication is also important when asking for help in online forums.

- Time management. The first few costumes you make will inevitably be finished last minute, the night before the convention. But as you continue, your time management will improve, and you'll be able to plan your costumes in advance.

- Money management. Cosplay can be expensive if you're not careful. You'll need to learn how to budget for all the materials you need to construct your costume, as well as the miscellaneous pieces (like shoes, hats, ears, etc.).

Emily Joice, "Cosplay as a Hobby: Learn Useful Skills and Improve Mental Health," *Cosplay Advice*, June 30, 2021. https://cosplayadvice.com.

At a 2023 festival in Los Angeles, California, manga and anime enthusiasts display Dekocar designs such as this one, featuring a character from Demon Slayer*.*

sized decals depicting scenes from manga and anime, known as Dekocar designs. "The draw for Dekocar enthusiasts is to effectively turn their vehicle into a rolling tribute to their favorite anime, manga, or Japanese video game property," says Andrew Beckford, a writer for *Motor Trend* magazine. He adds, "This usually involves having an elaborate custom vinyl wrap designed and placed on the vehicle."[30] There are even car shows where Dekocar enthusiasts can show off their vehicles and other manga and anime fans can admire them.

Fads come and go, but it seems that otaku culture—the love of manga, anime, and all things Japanese—is here to stay. That is because unlike other fads, it is based on something enduring: an art form with deep roots in Japanese culture, universal characters and themes, and dedicated artists who devote their lives to telling stories of human love, strength, and survival in a hostile universe.

> "The draw for Dekocar enthusiasts is to effectively turn their vehicle into a rolling tribute to their favorite anime, manga, or Japanese video game property."[30]
>
> —Andrew Beckford, writer for *Motor Trend*

SOURCE NOTES

Introduction: A Niche No More

1. Quoted in Julianne Sun, "Anime Might Not Be Cool, but It's Definitely Getting Popular," North by Northwestern, April 19, 2021. https://northbynorthwestern.com.
2. Jaryd Garcia, interview with the author, March 23, 2023.
3. Garcia, interview.
4. Quoted in Sun, "Anime Might Not Be Cool, but It's Definitely Getting Popular."
5. Quoted in Sun, "Anime Might Not Be Cool, but It's Definitely Getting Popular."

Chapter One: The Origins of an Art Form

6. George Bailey Sansom, *Japan: A Short Cultural History*. Stanford, CA: Stanford University Press, 1978, p. 253.
7. Quoted in Reuters, "Japan Finds Films by Early 'Anime' Pioneers," March 26, 2008. www.reuters.com.

Chapter Two: The Emergence of a Style

8. William Butler Yeats, *The Collected Works in Verse and Prose of William Butler Yeats,* Vol. 4, Project Gutenberg, August 5, 2015. www.gutenberg.org.
9. Miranda Barrientos, "The Relationship Between Japanese Theatre & *Spirited Away*," *Hayao Miyazaki* (blog), May 19, 2022. https://remnantisland.org.
10. Eric C. Rath, *The Ethos of Noh: Actors and Their Art*. Cambridge, MA: Harvard East Asian Monographs, 2004, p. 13.
11. Illya Szilak, "Filming 'Rae' for Atomic Vacation," *Illya Szilak* (blog), August 30, 2016. https://illyaszilak.com.
12. Quoted in Frank Bramlett, ed., *Linguistics and the Study of Comics*. London: Palgrave Macmillan, 2012, p. 92.
13. Quoted in Dennis Kennedy, ed., *The Oxford Encyclopedia of Theatre and Performance*, vol. 2. Oxford, UK: Oxford University Press, 2003, pp. 947–48.

Chapter Three: Rise of the Giant Robots

14. Quoted in Frederik L. Schodt, *Astro Boy Essays*. Berkeley, CA: Stone Bridge, 2006, p. 20.

15. Quoted in Schodt, *Astro Boy Essays*, p. 21.
16. Quoted in Kevin Kwong, "The Invincible Mazinger Z," *South China Morning Post* (Hong Kong), March 11, 2002. www.scmp.com.
17. Quoted in Jeff Blagdon, "Rise of the Giant Robots: How One Japanese Cartoon Spawned a Genre," The Verge, December 13, 2012. www.theverge.com.
18. Quoted in Blagdon, "Rise of the Giant Robots."
19. Michael Toole, "A-Mazinger Stories," Anime News Network, September 21, 2014. www.animenewsnetwork.com.

Chapter Four: Big Screen Success

20. Scott Cain, "'Transformers' a Bleak Toy Commercial Mutant," *Atlanta Constitution*, August 12, 1986. www.newspapers.com.
21. Jack Zink, "An Animated, Heavy-Metal Comic Book," *South Florida Sun Sentinel* (Deerfield Beach, FL), August 15, 1986. www.newspapers.com.
22. Roger Ebert, *"Pokemon: The First Movie," Chicago Sun-Times*, November 10, 1999. www.rogerebert.com.
23. Adrian Ruiz, "'Dragon Ball Super: Super Hero' Is a Love Letter," But Why Tho?, August 11, 2022. https://butwhytho.net.

Chapter Five: The Fun of Fandom

24. Quoted in Julie Beck, "What Fan Fiction Teaches That the Classroom Doesn't," *The Atlantic*, October 1, 2019. www.theatlantic.com.
25. Quoted in Beck, "What Fan Fiction Teaches That the Classroom Doesn't."
26. Admin, "Some Cosplay Ideas That Are Popular and Relevant for 2023," *Anime Costume Blog*, February 10, 2023. www.animecustome.com.
27. Quoted in Safa Warsi and Robert T. Muller, "Becoming Another Person Through Cosplay," *Talking About Trauma* (blog), *Psychology Today*, December 2, 2021. www.psychologytoday.com.
28. Quoted in Warsi and Muller, "Becoming Another Person Through Cosplay."
29. Quoted in Charlie Clark, "Cosplay Industry Grows Rapidly, Arizona Benefits from Pop Culture Phenomenon," Cronkite News, May 25, 2017. https://cronkitenews.azpbs.org.
30. Andrew Beckford, "Dekocar Phenomenon: Anime and Manga Fans Turn Their Cars into Heroic Canvases," *Motor Trend*, August 18, 2022. www.motortrend.com.

Books

Jonathan Clements, *Anime: A History*. 2nd ed. London: British Film Institute, 2023.

Paul Gravett, *Mangasia: The Definitive Guide to Asian Comics*. London: Thames & Hudson, 2017.

Raz Greenberg, *Hayao Miyazaki: Exploring the Early Work of Japan's Greatest Animator*. New York: Bloomsbury Academic, 2018.

Robert Henderson, *Quick Guide to Anime and Manga*. San Diego, CA: ReferencePoint, 2022.

Brigitte Koyama-Richard, *One Thousand Years of Manga*. London: Thames & Hudson, 2022.

Remi Lopez, *The Impact of Akira: A Manga (R)evolution*. Toulouse, France: Third Editions, 2021.

Susan Napier, *Miyazakiworld*. New Haven, CT: Yale University Press, 2018.

Bradley Steffens, *The Art and Artists of Anime*. San Diego, CA: ReferencePoint, 2022.

Akira Toriyama, *Dragon Ball: A Visual History*. San Francisco, CA: VIZ Media, 2019.

DVD

Arakawa Kaku, director, *Never-Ending Man: Hayao Miyazaki*, trans. David Crandall. Tokyo: NHK, 2017.

Internet Sources

Julie Beck, "What Fan Fiction Teaches That the Classroom Doesn't," *The Atlantic*, October 1, 2019. www.theatlantic.com.

Craig Elvy, "No Other Anime Will Ever Emulate *Dragon Ball*'s Success," Screen Rant, February 14, 2020. https://screenrant.com.

Matija Ferjan, "20+ Anime Statistics & Facts: How Many People Watch Anime?," Headphones Addict, February 1, 2023. https://headphonesaddict.com.

Will Heath, "20 Best Female Manga Artists You Need to Know," Japan Objects, October 9, 2020. https://japanobjects.com.

IGN Staff, "Top 25 Best Anime Series of All Time," IGN, September 22, 2022. www.ign.com.

Interac Network, "Otaku Culture in Japan—Japanese Anime, Manga, Idols & Video Games," November 24, 2021. https://interacnetwork.com.

Juha, "World's Best Anime and Manga Artists Ever," Okuha, March 13, 2020. https://okuha.com.

Mona, "Who's Hajime Isayama? Here's Why *Attack on Titan* Became One of the Best Manga," Otashift, June 25, 2019. www.otashift-tokyo.com.

Susana Polo, "Does Hayao Miyazaki Hate the Father of Manga?," Polygon, May 27, 2020. www.polygon.com.

Jacob Robinson, "Anime Coming to Netflix in 2023 and Beyond," What's on Netflix, March 24, 2023. www.whats-on-netflix.com.

Cheryl Teh, "It's Been 20 Years Since the Oscar-Winning Animated Movie 'Spirited Away' Was Released. Here Are 5 Ways It Changed Japanese Animation Forever," Insider, July 21, 2021. www.insider.com.

Websites

Anime News Network
www.animenewsnetwork.com
News, reviews, and feature reports on anime, manga, video games, and brief biographies of manga and anime artists.

Cosplay Advice
https://cosplayadvice.com
A fan-made site that offers tips and photos for making safe and realistic cosplay costumes and props.

***Dragon Ball* Official Site**
https://en.dragon-ball-official.com
Headquarters for all things *Dragon Ball*—news, product information, events, and videos. Includes a video newscast in Japanese with English subtitles covering *Dragon Ball* events of the week.

Studio Ghibli

www.ghibli.jp

The official website of the animation studio founded by Hayao Miyazaki. Includes information about new releases, stage productions, exhibitions, and upcoming events. Also includes a large library of colorful stills from the studio's animated classics, including *Spirited Away*.

Tezuka Osamu Official Website

www.tezukaosamu.net

A collection of items related to Tezuka, including a profile, a timeline of his life, photo albums, an animated short about his life (in Japanese only), and the wisdom he wanted to pass on to future generations in his "Message for Earth."

T.H.E.M. Anime Reviews

www.themanime.org

A website that offers up-to-date reviews of anime in all forms, including movies, television, and direct-to-video releases. Includes a huge, searchable archive of past reviews, arranged in alphabetical order by title. Also hosts message boards on a wide range of topics.

TV Tropes

https://tvtropes.org

A wiki edited and managed by its own audience, using a web browser. Includes entries on all aspects of popular culture, including manga and anime.

INDEX

ABOUT THE AUTHOR

Bradley Steffens is a novelist, poet, and award-winning author of more than sixty nonfiction books for children and young adults.